Celebrating Special Times

with Specia...

GLORIA GAITHER & SHIRLEY DOBSON

Artwork by Carrie Hartman

Multnomah Gifts®
Multnomah® Publishers *Sisters, Oregon*

CELEBRATING SPECIAL TIMES WITH SPECIAL PEOPLE

© 2005 by Gloria Gaither and James Dobson, Inc.
published by Multnomah Gifts®,
a division of Multnomah® Publishers, Inc.
P.O. Box 1720, Sisters, Oregon 97759

International Standard Book Number: 1-59052-397-0

Design by Koechel Peterson, & Assoc., Inc., Minneapolis, Minnesota

Artwork © 2005 by Carrie Hartman
www.carriehartman.com

Unless otherwise indicated, Scripture quotations are taken from:
The Holy Bible, New International Version ©1973, 1984 by International Bible Society, used by permission of
Zondervan Publishing House

Other Scripture quotations taken from: *Holy Bible*, New Living Translation (NLT) © 1996. Used by permission of
Tyndale House Publishers, Inc. All rights reserved. *The Living Bible* (TLB) © 1971. Used by permission of Tyndale
House Publishers, Inc. All rights reserved. *New American Standard Bible* (NASB) © 1960, 1977 by the Lockman
Foundation.

Vignettes written by Lisa Whelchel, Lee Hayes, Lynn D. Morrissey, and Janet Paschel used by permission.

Multnomah Publishers, Inc., has made every effort to provide proper and accurate source attribution for all
selections used in this book. Should any attribution be found to be incorrect, the publisher welcomes written
documentation supporting correction for subsequent printings. We gratefully acknowledge the cooperation of
other publishers and individuals who have granted permission for use of their material.

Multnomah is a trademark of Multnomah Publishers, Inc., and is registered in the U.S. Patent and Trademark
Office. The colophon is a trademark of Multnomah Publishers, Inc.

Printed in Belgium

For Information:
MULTNOMAH PUBLISHERS, INC. • P.O. BOX 1720 • SISTERS, OR 97759

05 06 07 08 09 10 11 12—11 10 9 8 7 6 5 4 3 2 1 0

To the villagers of my life who,
though they never traveled to exotic places,
taught me to discover joy right where I am
and to recognize the simple and sometimes hidden wonders
that come with each new dawn and every new moon.

—

GLORIA GAITHER

This book is
affectionately dedicated to
my husband, Jim Dobson, and to our children,
Danae and Ryan,
with whom we are sharing a lifetime
of priceless memories.

—

SHIRLEY DOBSON

Table of Contents

WHEN LOVE OVERFLOWING IS ALL THAT IS SHOWING

SAYING "I'M GLAD YOU'RE IN MY LIFE"

CONGRATULATIONS, GRADUATE

REASONS TO CELEBRATE THE SEASONS

MAKING MOVING MEMORIES

I love to take pictures. I'm by no means a professional photographer, but I love to memorize with my camera the magic moments that fill my heart with joy or overwhelm me with beauty.

Recently it began to dawn on me that the pictures I end up actually putting into scrapbooks or enlarging to frame always have people in them. Oh, they may have a glacier "calving" in the background or the wide hills of Wyoming overshadowed by the snowcapped peaks of the Grand Tetons towering over the girls on horseback; but no moment, I've discovered, *is* truly a moment unless it's shared with someone I love.

Think of the moments frozen in *your* memory. There was that trip with Grandma to Florida when you were eight—you know, the first time you ever parasailed. And what about the Thanksgiving that it snowed so deep Uncle Danny had to come get you on the snowmobile? Do you have a picture of the first clambake you ever experienced? You probably remember, to this very day, your mom's friend from New England who taught you to layer sweet corn, clams, potatoes, and seaweed in a pail and to boil everything over a buried fire pit on the beach.

I remember breaking Clela Howard's cake plate on the sidewalk that my mother trusted me to return, and how she enfolded me with forgiveness. I can tell you every detail of the sledding parties our youth group used to throw on Dixon Hill—there was always a huge bonfire, plenty of hot chocolate, and lots of laughter. I can describe the cedar smell of the cabin my parents used to rent in the Michigan woods, and I can list the name of every fish we would bring home after dark to clean and fry and eat at midnight with golden squares of corn bread.

But in every pictured memory there are people: family, friends, cousins, visitors, neighbors, children, grandparents…and a few surprises. I have also discovered as an adult that most of the memories I thought "just happened" were actually loving gifts to me from the people in my life. At the time, I thought the craft shelves just came with supplies, that vacations just rolled around every summer, and that hot dogs, baked beans, carrot and celery sticks, and homemade brownies just appeared at campfires.

In every photograph I shuffle through, there should also be "ghosted" images of those I never knew—people who taught my mother to make corn bread and who showed my dad how to start a fire by making a spark ignite dry leaves in the woods. There should be shadows of people like my grandmother, who sewed a canvas cover to the rib bones of a wagon to cross the country, making do and making magic for a generation of children that became my mentors.

But making memories in the computer age of the postmodern era—or any era, for that matter—will still be carved out of concern, painted in passion, and woven on a loom strung with love and creative imagination. Some of the materials we use will be new products of the information age, but most will be simple things at hand, the same things loving hands used to make the memories captured in the photos of our minds.

Before you begin reading the pages of this book, may I suggest that you pause briefly to think about the people who mean the most to you? Take this moment amid the breathless pace of living to recall the warmest experiences you have shared together with your loved ones—reliving the laughter, the joy, and the special occasions that made your hearts beat as one. I'm sure you'll agree that those golden memories with family, friends, and especially with children represent the most priceless treasures in your possession. When woven together in their intricate design, they compose the tapestry of your life. I can tell you they will only become more meaningful with the passage of time.

My grandmother used to sing an old folk song called "Precious Memories," which brought tears to our eyes. We sang it at her funeral because of the meaning it held for her. The lyrics were simple but powerful. The chorus read, "Precious memories, how they linger, how they ever flood my soul; in the stillness of the midnight, precious, sacred scenes unfold." The longer I live, the better I understand the deep sentiment that welled up within this aging matriarch as she sang about the things she loved dearly. I now comprehend something else. Precious memories are most easily captured while we are young. Like faded old photographs that remind us of the fresh-faced people we used to be, our memories of happy days with loved ones must be "constructed" in their own place and time. Not one of them can be recreated by those who look back wistfully, and perhaps regretfully, from afar.

For more than a decade, psychologists and researchers have been studying the elusive experience known as "happiness." In an attempt to ascertain what gives human beings the greatest satisfaction, they measured the impact of success, youth, good looks, achievement, prosperity, possessions, and framed credentials hanging on the wall. The clear winner was "supportive, intimate connections with other people," said psychologist David Myers in his book, *The Pursuit of Happiness*. Next came strong marriages, followed by meaningful religious faith.

Myers concluded, "If you can say that you're married to your 'best friend,' chances are that you've described not just your marriage, but your whole life."

If this understanding is accurate, and we certainly believe that it is, then why do we not give priority to the people in our lives? Why do we invest our limited days on this earth in the pursuit of that which does not satisfy the soul? King Solomon wrote of this folly in the book of Ecclesiastes and concluded that these worldly pursuits represent a "chasing after the wind." In the long run, he said, they amount to little more than vanity.

Clearly, our relationship with Jesus Christ and with our family, friends, and loved ones should be the focal point of our lives. But time is of the essence, particularly with regard to children. There is a brief window of opportunity when they are young that must be seized before it passes into history. In the blink of an eye, that era will be gone. It will be important to cultivate relationships throughout our lives, of course, but the responsibility to "seal the deal" with our kids will last but a moment. Everything that follows it will be based on the interactions occurring early on. The words we exchanged, the behavior we modeled, the games we played, the meals we shared, and yes, the occasional tears we shed will determine how we "see" each other in years to come. We must be intentional about the planning and execution of our experiences together.

It is with those thoughts in mind that Gloria and I have assembled some ideas to serve as a springboard for use as you mark important accomplishments, birthdays, and other passages during your children's journey toward adulthood. We've also included suggestions to help you cultivate in your family the value of reaching out with Jesus' love to relatives, church members, and neighbors. While the circumstances and participants in each of your memory-making efforts will vary, the constant that will always make it special is that you and your loved ones will be giving the gift of yourselves! The ideas we offer in this book require little expense, preparation, or time. The ball is now in your court. Let's not miss today's opportunities to create "precious memories" that will *linger* and unfold as we journey together through this parenting experience.

Remembering Mom on Your Birthday

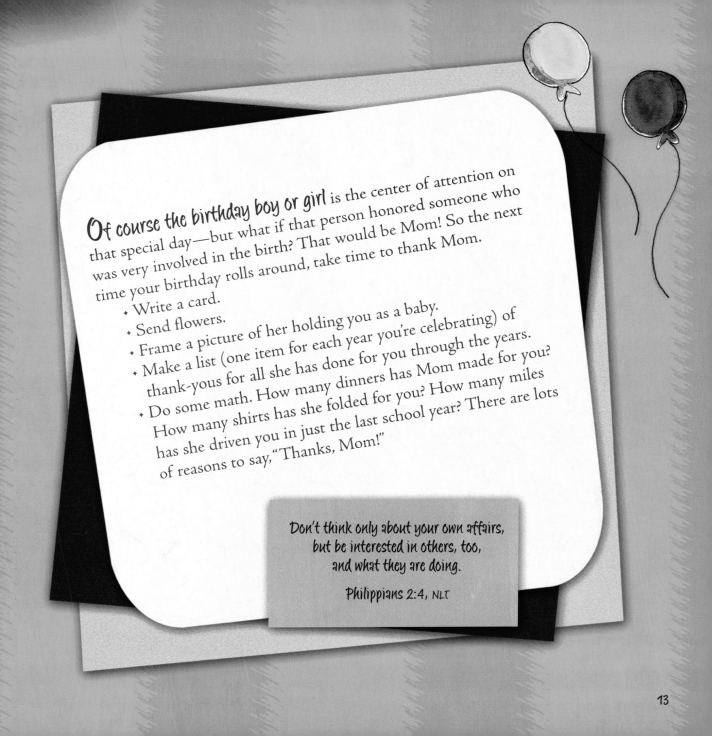

Of course the birthday boy or girl is the center of attention on that special day—but what if that person honored someone who was very involved in the birth? That would be Mom! So the next time your birthday rolls around, take time to thank Mom.

+ Write a card.
+ Send flowers.
+ Frame a picture of her holding you as a baby.
+ Make a list (one item for each year you're celebrating) of thank-yous for all she has done for you through the years.
+ Do some math. How many dinners has Mom made for you? How many shirts has she folded for you? How many miles has she driven you in just the last school year? There are lots of reasons to say, "Thanks, Mom!"

Don't think only about your own affairs,
but be interested in others, too,
and what they are doing.

Philippians 2:4, NLT

"Honor your father and mother"—which is the first commandment with a promise—"that it may go well with you and that you may enjoy long life on the earth."

Ephesians 6:2-3

Say, "Happy Anniversary!" by doing what you can to help a second (or third!) honeymoon happen.

- Find out where your parents honeymooned and whether they would like to go back—or where they'd like to go for the first time.
- Collect travel brochures advertising that special spot. Those four-color photos can help you sell the idea to your parents.
- Make it easier for Mom and Dad to leave by cooperating with babysitting plans if you're on the young side or by helping with the finances if you're older. You might, for instance, hold a garage sale to raise money for their trip. Or give up a regular treat (that daily latte or the Sunday morning doughnuts) and put the money into the "Second Honeymoon Fund."
- Join financial forces with your brothers and sisters to buy your folks something special for their trip. New luggage? A nightgown or some perfume for Mom? Some cologne or a new swimsuit for Dad?
- Need a less complicated plan? Make an anniversary dinner for Mom and Dad. The food can be simple, but let the wording on an elegant computer-generated menu class it up. (Who would dream that "pasta in a light cream sauce" came from a box?) Light some candles, put on soft music, and let Mom and Dad celebrate being husband and wife.
- Schedule a love-song-a-gram for the special couple. During their kid-made anniversary dinner or as they leave on that special trip, have some students from the local high school choir arrive with flowers or balloons and a special song. Do you know "their" song? A favorite hymn or praise song? A song that has meant something to them at some point? This serenade will be a special touch for a remarkable couple's momentous time.

There's nothing better for kids of any age than having parents who love each other. And honoring your parents in ways like this can help fuel that love.

Keeping Love Alive

Keep your love for husband or wife
alive with some of these options:

• Is your anniversary on June 29? Then on the twenty-ninth of every month, celebrate your marriage. Men, take home a rose. Wives, put a love note in your husband's lunch box. Go out for the evening—or have dinner at home, but use the china you got as wedding presents.

• Add romance to an overnight trip or a vacation-for-two by taking along a candle and candleholder. That simple touch can add romance to any hotel room or camper. At bedtime, light the candle and enjoy the restful, soothing atmosphere.

• What is "your" song? If you don't have one, have fun choosing one—and finding a recording of it and even learning to play it on whatever instrument you've mastered.

• Dad, a simple thank-you kiss for Mom after a meal not only expresses your gratitude to her, but it tells the kids that their parents love and appreciate each other.

+ On your way home from work, Dad, pick up some bath crystals. Let her know that this little gift comes with the promise that you'll take the kids whenever she wants to leisurely enjoy it.

+ Before Mom and your new baby arrive home from the hospital, write a love note to your bride and leave it on her pillow. In the note, welcome your wife and your child home, tell them of your love for them, and let them know what a joy and privilege it is to be their husband and father. Don't be surprised if Mom cherishes this special note for years to come.

Give honor to marriage, and remain faithful to one another in marriage.

Hebrews 13:4, NLT

Dad, You're Up!

"The LORD bless you and keep you;
the LORD make his face shine upon you
and be gracious to you;
the LORD turn his face toward you
and give you peace."

Numbers 6:24-25

Dads and kids can share a special bond. Here are some ways to strengthen that bond.

- Pack a picnic lunch for you and your kids and head for a surprise destination. (Can you top this? When one dad took his gang to the beach, their meal consisted of Red Vines, bananas, and chips!)
- Shopping can often be Mom's job, so pull a switcheroo and take charge. Make it your and your child's quest to find something specific: a model to build together, a new dress, new shoes, the first baseball mitt or basketball. Have lunch together afterward—or at least make time for an ice-cream cone!
- Plan a special outing with another dad and daughter or dad and son. Go to a ball game, car race, or movie. Take a fishing trip, go mountain climbing, or share a favorite hike.
- Take charge of family movie night. Rent a movie of your choice from the library or a video rental store—or spend the evening looking at movies you took of the kids when they were younger.
- What can you do to wake up the kids every morning in a unique and special way? Would a back rub work? Make up a silly wake-up song. Or open the curtains and declare with joy, "This is the day the Lord hath made!"

Close your children's day with a special blessing. You could quote Numbers 6:24–26 ("The LORD bless you and keep you; the LORD make his face shine upon you and be gracious to you; the LORD turn his face toward you and give you peace") or say something like "May God help you grow up to be a great man/woman of God who loves God with all his/her heart."

Love Letters to a Little One

There's nothing quite like that rush of first love when you lay eyes on a newborn family member. Savor—and preserve—that moment by writing a love letter to that precious little person. And consider doing this regularly: on every birthday, every half-birthday, even every month.

- Let your baby know what a blessing she is—and why.
- Tell him the joy you're feeling in welcoming him to the world or watching him grow over the past year.
- Share things about yourself and your family history that you would like the child to know and even pass along someday.
- Mention current world and national events.
- Talk about things you're learning about the Lord and things you want her to be sure to learn about Him.
- Most of all, affirm your love for this precious blessing.

Imagine your child being able to read such encouraging words when he or she is feeling discouraged, unlovable, lonely, or afraid. If you make a point of writing love letters regularly and keeping them together, that child will have a concrete "I love you!" to cherish and lean on through the years.

> You show that you are a letter from Christ…written not with ink but with the Spirit of the living God, not on tablets of stone but on tablets of human hearts.
>
> 2 Corinthians 3:3

Dear Emily,
I want
you to know
how me

A Living Mirror of Growth

Celebrate the birth of a child by planting a tree, an ornamental fruit tree, or a rose bush that will grow as the baby grows. Or make a tradition of planting a tree for each child in the family when they reach a certain age.

Besides a camera to document the special tree-planting event, you'll need:

A young tree (either a home-grown seedling or a balled-and-burlapped tree from a nursery)

Spades

A small bag of peat moss

Water

A fertilizer spike formulated for the type of tree you choose

+ Choose a site for the tree that will allow plenty of room for healthy growth and spreading. Your nurseryman can let you know how much space your tree needs.
+ Dig a hole approximately one-and-one-half times as wide and as deep as the balled roots or twice as large as the root system of a seedling. Take turns digging. Be sure to let younger children help.
+ Sprinkle a good layer of peat moss in the bottom of the hole.
+ Set the tree into the hole, letting the bottom of the roots touch the peat moss. If the roots are not balled, be sure to gently spread them. Take care to see that the roots are not broken or crowded.
+ Check to see that the crown of the root system or the top of the balled roots is just slightly lower than the top surface of the ground.
+ Fill the hole half full of water.
+ Sprinkle loose soil into the hole until the hole is filled. As you fill it, form around the tree trunk, at ground level, a sort of saucer that will hold water.

+ Carefully water the tree again, filling the saucer but not so full that it runs over. As the water seeps in, it will naturally pack the soil around the roots so you do not need to press the soil down and run the danger of breaking the tender roots. After the water has seeped in, you may need to add a little more soil, but be sure to maintain the saucer.
+ Insert the fertilizer spike just inside the rim of the soil saucer.
+ Water each day by filling the saucer with water until the tree has a good start. Then water it whenever the weather is dry.

If you plant the trees when your children are older, give them the responsibility of keeping their own tree watered.

Let each tree you plant remind you to pray for your children and to thank God for the joy of working with Him to raise them.

As your children grow, tell them about their own tree. Explain that it was planted by those who love them most in celebration of their birth and in great anticipation of their growth. When the children are old enough to understand, talk about what a tree needs to grow, what they themselves need in order to grow, and what we all need in order to become the people God wants us to be. Talk, too, about the demands of the different seasons and about the different seasons in a person's life. Let your children know that you are there to help nurture them through every season of their life.

If you want to branch off...

+ From time to time, take pictures of the tree's growth.
+ After the tree begins to mature, take pictures of it in different seasons.
+ When your children are old enough, encourage them to write about the tree.

The resulting journal will be a special reflection of your child's growth. You might even combine these photos with "Love Letters" to your child (see page 20).

A Baby Banner Blessing

"Welcome to the Fortner Family!"

"Welcome Home, Megan!"

"Building Site: Stephen Will Be Growing Here!"

"We're So Glad You're Part of the Family, Kristin!"

Even though the newest addition (born or adopted into the family) can't read, making a baby banner is a great activity for Dad and older siblings.

+ Purchase a large sheet of poster board or a length of butcher paper.

+ Spread a protective layer of newspapers on the garage floor or driveway.

+ Let the children design the poster and choose the words.

+ Use a pencil to sketch the message and drawings onto the banner—or let your home-computer technology help you. Many programs can help you make colorful banners.

+ Use markers or tempera paint to add color to the poster.

+ Work together to clean up.

Hang the banner over the crib in the nursery or, at least initially, on the garage door for Baby's grand arrival home.

"Any of you who welcomes a little child like this because you are mine, is welcoming me and caring for me."

Matthew 18:5, TLB

From the Heart of God's Word

It's an amazing privilege to raise a child up to know the Lord—and it's never too early to start. So start now by dedicating a Scripture verse to Baby. You could choose a verse of...

- **Promise**...like Jeremiah 29:11
- **Hope**...like Isaiah 40:11
- **Inspiration**...like Isaiah 40:30–31
- **Instruction**...like Proverbs 3:5–6 or Mark 12:30–31
- **Truth**...like John 14:6
- **Gospel**...like John 3:16

Whatever verse you choose, write it in calligraphy and frame it or have it printed on a plaque. Hang it in Baby's room and pray it over him or her often.

Jesus said unto him, "I am the Way, the Truth, and the Life, no man cometh unto the Father but by me". John 14:6

Train a child in the way he should go,
and when he is old
he will not turn from it.

Proverbs 22:6

26

It's a Baby Doll Shower!

When my daughter, Clancy, turned three, she asked for a brand-new baby doll for her birthday. It was humbling to realize that my baby wanted to be a mommy just like me. It appeared she had inherited more than my smile and olive skin. She was already acting just like I did as an expectant mother.

I recognized myself in her when she began asking for baby doll clothes before she was even "showing." Weeks before her birthday, she was shopping for baby beds and high chairs and a diaper bag in the newspaper's Toys "R" Us flier. She couldn't write, but she was making a mental list of all the stuff her baby was going to need when it arrived. I thought to myself, *Boy, this baby is going to end up costing a lot more than $29.95.*

I decided right away that it was time to throw my daughter a baby doll shower! I sent out beautiful invitations to all of her little girlfriends. I translated Clancy's baby "registry" list and stuffed it in the envelope along with a swatch of pastel fabric.

When the other little mommies arrived, they were served fruit punch in baby bottles with their names written on them with puffy markers. They played games like "who can change a diaper fastest?" and "guess the flavor in the baby food jar."

It was soon time to unwrap her gifts. Clancy received diapers, dresses, bottles, blankets, a Snugli, a stroller—more than her little baby could ever need or use. Just like a real shower!

The grand finale was the delivery of her brand-new baby girl. As Clancy held her close and rocked her adoringly, I was caught off guard by a wave of understanding: In a few too many way-too-fast years, my baby would grow up and be a mommy just like me.

by Lisa Whelchel

It's Shower Time!

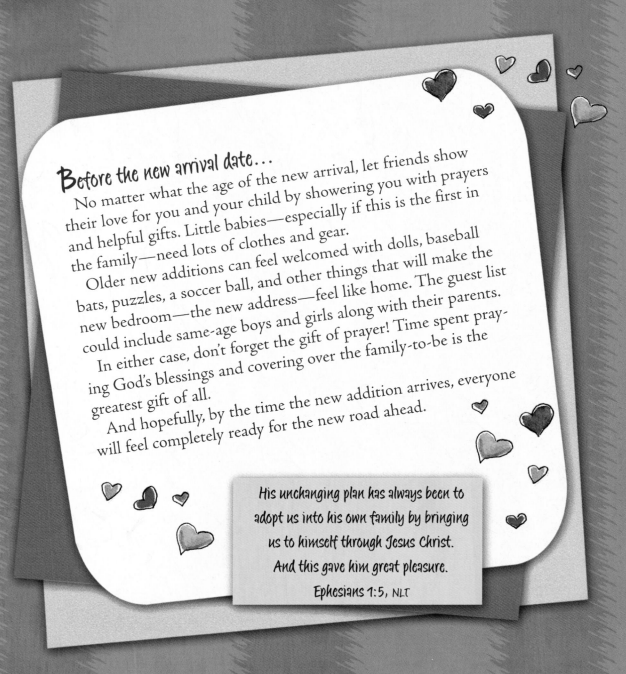

Before the new arrival date…

No matter what the age of the new arrival, let friends show their love for you and your child by showering you with prayers and helpful gifts. Little babies—especially if this is the first in the family—need lots of clothes and gear.

Older new additions can feel welcomed with dolls, baseball bats, puzzles, a soccer ball, and other things that will make the new bedroom—the new address—feel like home. The guest list could include same-age boys and girls along with their parents.

In either case, don't forget the gift of prayer! Time spent praying God's blessings and covering over the family-to-be is the greatest gift of all.

And hopefully, by the time the new addition arrives, everyone will feel completely ready for the new road ahead.

His unchanging plan has always been to adopt us into his own family by bringing us to himself through Jesus Christ. And this gave him great pleasure.

Ephesians 1:5, NLT

New Friends for an Older Adopted Child

After there's been an appropriate amount of time for adjustment and if language allows, invite the Sunday school class (and the teacher) from your church into your home for pizza and a movie. Or have a handful of classmates from the new school over to build tacos and play games.

If your child is from another country, use this opportunity to educate the new friends. Have decorations and photos that reflect the child's first country, as well as some dishes representing that country's regional cuisine, so that classmates can get to know their new friend's world.

A get-to-know-each-other game (see ideas on following page) might be a great idea.

Getting to Know You

• "My Name Is…": Go around the circle and introduce yourselves by saying your name and something about you that starts with the same first letter as your name. Give guests a category like favorite food ("My name is Pam, and I love pizza") or favorite activity ("My name is Sarah, and soccer is my favorite sport"). The first person says her name and something about herself. The second person reintroduces the first person and introduces himself as well. The third person reintroduces the first and second people, and then introduces herself…. You see the pattern. Needless to say, the game gets more challenging as you go along!

• The Animal Kingdom: A slight variation on the theme above invites guests to introduce themselves and say that they're like a certain animal because of a specific trait: "I'm like a hyena because I love to laugh"; "I'm like a cheetah because I can run pretty fast"; "I'm like a bird because I like to sing."

• "Bingo!": Make a grid of twenty-five squares. Inside each square write a fact ("Has blue eyes"; "Likes brussels sprouts"; "Is one of three kids in the family"; "Owns a fish"; "Doesn't like chocolate"; etc.). Then set the gang loose to find someone in the crowd who is described by an unclaimed fact on the grid. That person signs her name in the box with a phrase that describes her. The first person to score a bingo—by getting five signatures in a row vertically, horizontally, or diagonally—hollers "Bingo!"

An Annual Celebration

Everyone has a birthday, but only special people have an adoption day—and that's definitely worth celebrating! What traditions would you like to establish?

- Look at photos or view a video you made on his arrival day. Notice how he's grown over the past year and talk about how glad you are that God blessed your family with his presence.
- Let the special family member know what she brings to the family that you can't imagine being without. Is it that radiant smile, her unique perspective on life, a good way with siblings, commitment to the family, helpfulness around the house, the infectious laugh, or something else?
- What have you learned about being family since your adopted child came to live with you? Let everyone—including the honoree—answer the question.
- If you adopted a child from another culture, this day could be a time to celebrate with a favorite meal from that first homeland.
- Have a family time of worship and thanksgiving. Praise God for bringing all of you together. Thank Him for choosing you for one another.

Everyone who believes that Jesus is the Christ is a child of God. And everyone who loves the Father loves his children, too.

1 John 5:1, NLT

Grandparents' Day

What can you do to say, "I love you" in a special and maybe unexpected way on September 9?

- If Grandma and Grandpa are close, how 'bout a surprise visit? Or whisk them away for a special meal at your house!
- Have Mom or Dad take a picture of all you grandkids. Get it developed. Mount it with a wide enough mat so that you can write, "We love you, Grandma and Grandpa!" and sign your names.
- What are some of Grandma's favorite things to do with you? Make a date to do one of those.
- What does Grandpa like to talk to you about? Set apart some time to listen.
- What is one of your most favorite memories of time with Grandma and/or Grandpa? Let them know with a drawing, a photo, or a thank-you note.
- "I love you, Grandma/Grandpa, because…" could be the beginning of a note that special person will long treasure.

> Their first responsibility is to show godliness at home and repay their parents by taking care of them. This is something that pleases God very much.
> 1 Timothy 5:4, NLT

August 10

Last weekend I went to my grandma and grandpa's cabin. They have thirteen acres. The first day we were there we had a camp fire with my cousins. The second day we all got up and went into the woods. We swung from grape vines and walked across water on log bridges. It was really fun. It took two whole hours. My grandma says that the woods are a magical. Then we all took a nap.

Lee Hayes

No one tells stories like Grandma or Grandpa—and often their grandkids are avid fans. So ask grandparents to share with their grandchildren details about their own growing-up years. Feel free to eavesdrop and take notes so that the family heritage will not be lost.

+ What chores did the grandparents have to do when they were growing up?
+ When they were young, what did Grandpa and Grandpa like to do after their chores were done?
+ What were the grandparents' favorite toys?
+ What meal was special to each of them?
+ What family tradition did Grandma and Grandpa enjoy as children—and is it still being done in the family today? If not, could it be?
+ What favorite and/or eccentric relative does the next generation definitely need to learn about? Give all the details.

Gather the family after the evening meal (on as many evenings as necessary and/or possible) for a time to listen to the older generation talk about their lives. And don't forget to explore the Internet to both confirm and discover more about your family's roots.

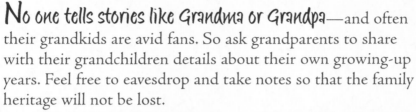

Remember the days of old; consider the generations long past. Ask your father and he will tell you, your elders, and they will explain to you.

Deuteronomy 32:7

Grand Times with Grandkids

- Grandma and Grandpa, when you visit your grandchildren, be sure to tell them about something that was part of your life when you were their age but is not part of their life today. You might talk about how things were done (did you really grow your own vegetables and even milk cows?), tools and equipment you or your parents used (there weren't computers?!), or a typical school day (how much homework did you have?). Be sure your grandkids know how you met each other and even why you said "I do."
- Do your grandchildren live close enough for you to share a meal with them once a week? If so, choose Saturday breakfast, Sunday dinner, or the Tuesday after-school snack. If the kids are farther away, think about sharing a phone call once a week. Schedule the meal or the phone call for the same time each week. Kids love routines and traditions.
- There's something so wonderful about sharing a book. So every time you're together, read! Keep a supply of storybooks at your home, and you might even take a favorite as a gift when you go to visit. Of course you'll do the reading when the kids are young, but as they grow, you can read aloud together.
- It's a game that doesn't need equipment. Simply have your young grandchildren identify your animal sounds. You might even switch roles and guess what animal they're being. Either way, you're sure to add the sound of laughter.
- Older children (ages seven to fifteen) might enjoy a bird-watching hike with you. Don't forget the binoculars and a good birding book. Or let the Internet help you out.

- A nature hike would be fun, too. When do the wildflowers bloom? What animals might you see if you go at dusk? Where's a good spot for a sunrise hike? Be creative! Again, the Internet can be a great resource before you set out.
- Older children (twelve and above) would probably love a trip to the theater, symphony, or ballet with Grandpa and Grandma. Check to see if your community, or theirs, has special performances for young people. Some community children's theater makes for a delightful outing for even younger grandkids.

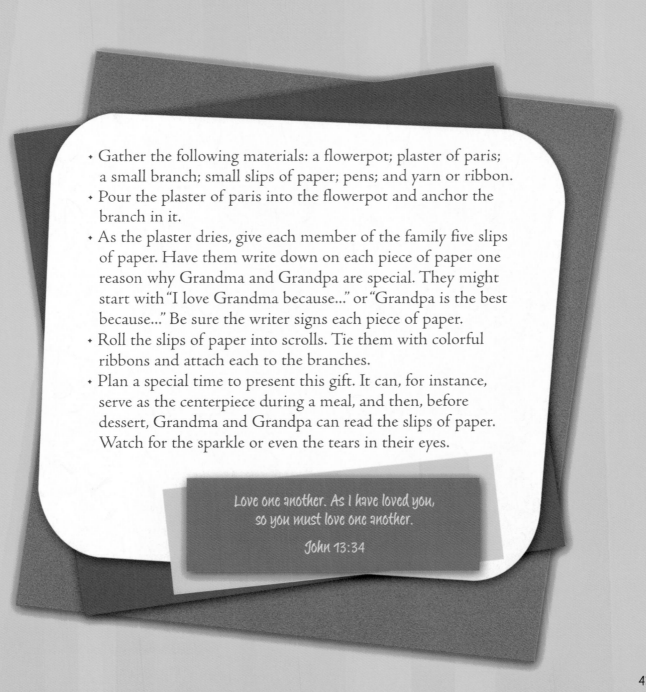

- Gather the following materials: a flowerpot; plaster of paris; a small branch; small slips of paper; pens; and yarn or ribbon.
- Pour the plaster of paris into the flowerpot and anchor the branch in it.
- As the plaster dries, give each member of the family five slips of paper. Have them write down on each piece of paper one reason why Grandma and Grandpa are special. They might start with "I love Grandma because…" or "Grandpa is the best because…" Be sure the writer signs each piece of paper.
- Roll the slips of paper into scrolls. Tie them with colorful ribbons and attach each to the branches.
- Plan a special time to present this gift. It can, for instance, serve as the centerpiece during a meal, and then, before dessert, Grandma and Grandpa can read the slips of paper. Watch for the sparkle or even the tears in their eyes.

Love one another. As I have loved you,
so you must love one another.

John 13:34

What's in a Name?

The grandkids might be surprised that Grandma and Grandpa have other names! Celebrate their names even as you celebrate them.

- On a large piece of poster board, write Grandma or Grandpa's first name in big block letters. You can arrange the letters vertically or horizontally. Then have the kids draw colorful pictures of that grandparent's favorite foods, clothes, hobbies, sports, or games—anything that reminds them of that very special person.
- Write Grandma or Grandpa's first name vertically and let it be an acrostic of love that the grandkids complete. For example:

    E: elegant, energetic
    L: loving, laughing
    S: smart, sweet
    A: admirable, adventurous

A Family Affair

Plan on Saturday-morning family time once a month to do something special for someone special.

+ Write a grandparent or a favorite aunt—just because. After all, "I love you" needn't be reserved for a special occasion.
+ Invite a favorite person—relative, neighbor, friend, coworker, church family—over for an easy meal. Make a large panful of taco meat and let folks build their own tacos or taco salad for lunch or dinner and fun.
+ Work on the family photo collection. That may mean making a fancy photo album, organizing a pictorial biography of your child's life, or simply sorting a long-neglected pile of pictures.
+ Whose birthday is next on the calendar? Let your kids get involved in celebrating a parent or sibling's big day.

Let us practice loving each other,
for love comes from God and those
who are loving and kind show that
they are children of God.

1 John 4:7, TLB

To Be a Man

My little nephew was playing on the floor with his trucks one fine spring morning. His grandma was standing at the sink washing a panful of fresh leaf lettuce, some of the first to be harvested in town.

"What are you going to be when you grow up?" his grandma asked.

David crawled across the floor, pushing his toy tractor and making motor noises with his mouth.

"Would you like working in a big factory or having an office of your own? Are you going to be a teacher? Or maybe a fireman or a policeman?"

David crawled closer to the back screen door, which was open to the pungent fragrance of freshly turned soil. He ran his little tractor up the earth with the garden tractor.

"Nope," he finally said. "I just wanna be a man, like my grandpa!"

Lord, our world is so in need of heroes. Give us fewer "professionals" and more men who stand tall in integrity and gentle strength and godliness. Thank You that a real one lives at our house. Amen.

by Gloria Gaither

Sharing the Colors of Spring

Add a touch of spring to your home and your neighborhood.

- The happy colors of marigolds, petunias, geraniums, impatiens, or other favorites can bring a garden to life. Start them from seeds or buy pony packs of young plants that are ready to go right into the ground.
- Brighten the day—and yard—of someone you love. As a family, work together to fill that person's outside planters, window boxes, or gardens with spring color. If necessary, purchase containers, fill them with flowers (see below), take along some cookies and lemonade when you deliver this gift of love, and welcome spring together.

A Quick How-To

1. Fill the container with soil and then mix in suitable fertilizer.
2. Carefully remove the plants from the pony pack(s) and arrange them in the container. Keep in mind the expected height and different colors of the flowers.
3. Water the newly transplanted flowers.

His righteousness will be like a garden in early spring,
filled with young plants springing up everywhere.

Isaiah 61:11, NLT

How to Be a "Block Head"!

A block party is a great way to get acquainted and to turn neighbors into friends. And don't be surprised if it becomes an annual or semiannual event in your neighborhood. Here's an idea for the first:

- Invite each family on your block to come to your house and bring their favorite dessert.
- Provide name tags (unless everyone already knows each other!) as well as paper goods, eating utensils, and beverages.
- Plan a get-acquainted or ice breaker mixer. (We've provided an idea on page 54.) If neighbors already know each other well, play charades, Pictionary, baseball, or volleyball.
- On a practical note, this initial block party is a great time to compile a neighborhood roster. Get names and ages of children, phone numbers for emergency situations, and any other information that might be helpful.

"Love your neighbor as yourself."

Matthew 19:19

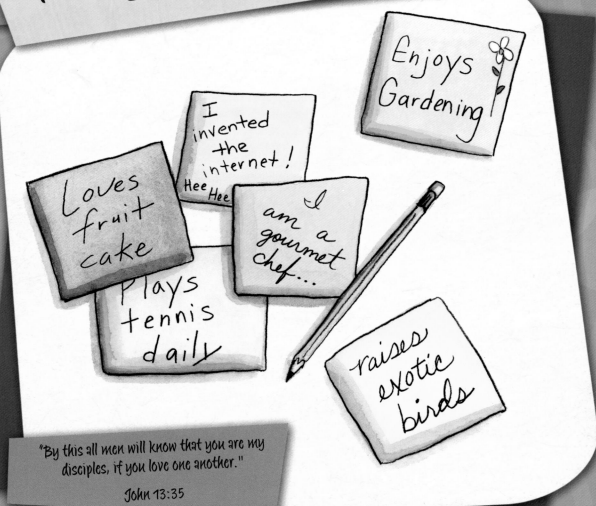

1. On a sheet of paper draw a grid of 1" x 2" squares. Have at least one square per guest.
2. At the top of each square write a characteristic that might apply to one of your guests. These can be humorous or not. You might even ask folks when they RSVP to share an interesting fact about themselves and then use those facts in your grid.
3. When guests arrive, give each of them a pencil and a copy of the chart. Give them a set time (fifteen minutes?) to circulate among the group, meeting as many people as possible and asking questions. Their goal is to put a name by each trait or fact.
4. When the allotted time is up, find out who has the most squares filled in. Ask the winner to read aloud the names and corresponding traits or facts, having each person stand as his or her name is called. If not all the guests are introduced this way, ask the remaining guests to stand and introduce themselves.

SAMPLE:
Talks back to TV commercials
Can wiggle ears
Can touch palms to floor
Hates chocolate
Runs two miles a day

Passing Friendship from Door to Door

Start a friendship basket for your neighborhood.

+ Buy a large, inexpensive basket.
+ Tie a bright ribbon on the handle along with directions: "We wanted you to know that it's great to have you as neighbors. Enjoy what's inside and then, within the next week or so, please put something special in this basket for the family next door."
+ Since you're starting the neighborhood fun, fill the basket with things that your next-door neighbors will enjoy. That might mean brownies, a gift certificate for the local video store and a few bags of microwave popcorn, a coupon for an evening of babysitting at your house or theirs, or a complete dinner (give the cook a heads-up!).
+ When the basket comes back to you, send it back in the opposite direction from its first trip.

Be devoted to one another in brotherly love. Honor one another above yourselves.

Romans 12:10

Love One Another...

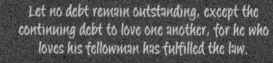

Let no debt remain outstanding, except the continuing debt to love one another, for he who loves his fellowman has fulfilled the law.

Romans 13:8

Do you have an older neighbor who would enjoy a visit or appreciate some help? Join together with a family member or friend and let them know you care. Here are some ideas:

- Invite your friend to join your family on a trip to the local ice cream parlor—or bring back a cone if that special person can't get out.
- Stop by to say hello during a family bike ride.
- Invite this neighbor to a family birthday party. Make sure there's a goodie bag for him.
- Offer—in a way that can't be refused!—to mow the grass, trim around the mailbox, pull some weeds, or even paint the fence.
- Mail this friend a Valentine's Day or Easter card.
- Share a recording (audio or video) of a concert, church service, school program, or band recital.
- Ask your friend's opinion of a paper, poem, or song you've written.
- Drop by your neighbor's house with a friend of yours. Keep your visit short.
- Get the whole family involved. Sweep the driveway or sidewalk, wash the car, clean the windows on the outside, shake the rugs, or run some errands for your neighbor.
- An older friend might appreciate you being "eyes" for them. Once or twice a week read to her—and encourage her to invite some friends to join you.
- Write and mail letters for your friend and help him pay his bills.
- Give a subscription to a large-print edition of a good magazine. Here are two ideas: Reader's Digest Fund for the Blind, Large-Type Publication, P.O. Box 241, Mt. Morris, IL 61054 and Guideposts, Big Print Edition, Carmel, NY 10512.

Do Unto Others

We all like to be appreciated, and mail deliverers, gardeners, police officers, firefighters, librarians, crossing guards, teachers, and pastors are no different. So say "thank you!" to folks like these who contribute to the well-being of your neighborhood. The list is limited only by your imagination.

+ On a hot summer day, share a cool glass of lemonade with the mail deliverer, the gardener, or the trash collector.
+ Take a batch of homemade cookies to the local fire station or police department.
+ If a neighbor is working hard outside, take over a cool drink and offer a helping hand for a bit.
+ Do a good deed together for a neighbor, pastor, or teacher. Be creative! Does the neighbor down the street need her lawn mown? How about baking brownies for the new family on the block? Invite a friend's kids over—and let your kids help entertain them—so she can have an hour to herself. Pull weeds from the church's lawn. Offer to help your child's teacher change bulletin boards.
+ Serve together at church. Can you stuff envelopes? Be greeters on Sunday morning? Help usher? If you don't know what needs to be done, ask your church secretary.
+ What mission opportunities does your church make available to you? Can your family serve at a soup kitchen? Can you donate a couple of backpacks full of school supplies for a needy family? Again, if you don't know what's available in your community, make phone calls and ask questions.

Remember that thoughtful gestures like these can do much to build good feelings in a neighborhood.

He will not forget your work and the love you have shown him as you have helped his people and continue to help them.

Hebrews 6:10

Saying "Get Well"

+ Make a "Leaves of Love" poster. On a piece of poster board, draw a large tree with bare limbs. Cut out ten to twenty leaves—each large enough to write on—from green construction paper. (If it's fall, you might make red, yellow, and orange leaves.) Have family members and friends write a love note, joke, or riddle on each leaf. Tape the leaves on the tree and hang this tree of encouragement in the patient's room where it can be easily read and enjoyed.
+ Instead of taking or sending candy and flowers, collect pictures of the patient's family. That might mean going to the house and taking photos. But know that the patient will love showing them to nurses and other friends who stop by. Your thoughtfulness and efforts will be much appreciated.

Blessed are those who mourn,
for they will be comforted.

Matthew 5:4

Blessed Are Those Who Comfort

Being sick is no fun. Help the time pass faster for your child with these acts of love and comfort:

- Read her favorite books to her.
- To soothe a fever, dampen a washcloth with cold water. Squeeze it out thoroughly and place it on your patient's forehead.
- Put a bell next to your patient's bed so he can let you know when he needs you.
- Sleep in the room with the child. Your presence will be a real source of comfort, especially if she may vomit. That can be frightening for a child.
- A favorite video or cd can be a good friend for a sick child.
- If your patient is up to it, let him talk briefly on the phone to someone he loves and misses.
- Go through baby pictures and family photo albums, something you probably don't do when your child is healthy and running around.

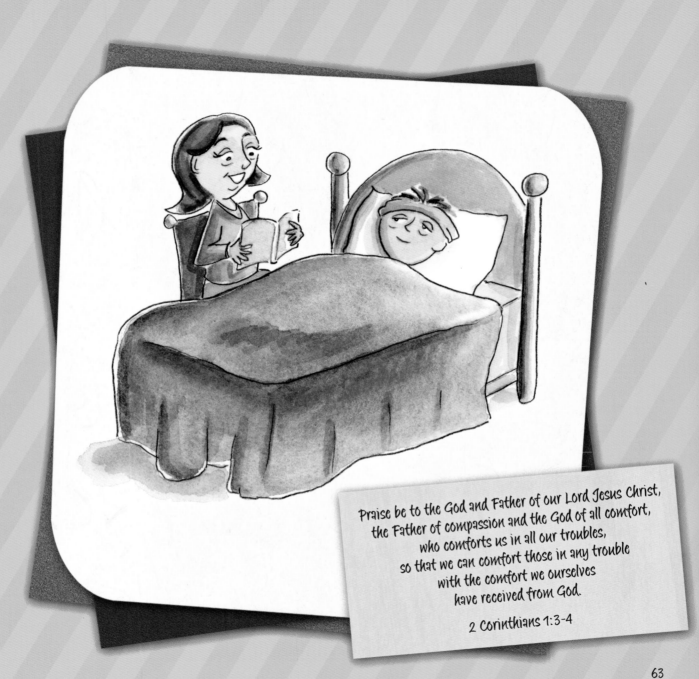

Praise be to the God and Father of our Lord Jesus Christ,
the Father of compassion and the God of all comfort,
who comforts us in all our troubles,
so that we can comfort those in any trouble
with the comfort we ourselves
have received from God.

2 Corinthians 1:3-4

Special Delivery for the Special Patient

If you have any encouragement from being united with Christ, if any comfort from his love, if any fellowship with the Spirit, if any tenderness and compassion, then make my joy complete by being like-minded, having the same love, being one in spirit and purpose.

Philippians 2:1-2

In case you've never noticed, it can be difficult to keep an active child as quiet as he needs to be during a minor illness or recuperation from something more serious. A lap table can be a big help.

- Make a lap table from a sturdy cardboard box. Cut arches out of it so that the box will fit over the child's legs.
- Spray paint the table with a bright color and let it dry thoroughly.
- Turn the lap table upside down. Place inside it a smaller box (shoe-box size works) that will be a busy box for those sick or slowed-down days.
- Fill the smaller box with craft and activity materials suitable for your patient:

Scissors
Paste or glue
Yarn, thread
Buttons, beads
Crayons or markers
Construction paper

Magazines with lots of pictures for cutting out
Stencils
Colored pencils, gel pens

Coloring books or how-to-draw books
Crossword puzzles or word searches
Letter-writing materials

Your patient can make collages, jigsaw puzzles, scrapbooks, drawings, and so much more—and she just *may* stay quiet for a while!

- Use the box and lap table only on sick days so that it's a special treat.

For Those with "Drawn Out" Recoveries

+ Send a small gift each day: an assortment of gum, a good book with a homemade bookmark, a bright and cheerful helium balloon, a package of quick-growing seeds to plant (lima beans and marigolds work well) along with a brightly painted flowerpot and potting soil, a miniature puzzle, a lollipop.... Be creative.
+ Fill a box with materials for drawing, making collages, and doing other art projects: scissors, colored pencils, paper, fabric, buttons, needles, thread, a magnifying glass, pieces of aluminum foil for making shapes, paper clips, modeling clay, a hole-punch, toothpicks, glue, gummed stars, stickers, beads and thread, watercolors.... Visiting a craft store will give you even more great ideas.
+ Plant a garden indoors. Place two or three pieces of dampened cotton in a glass. Push a grapefruit seed, a pea, or a bean into the cotton. Keep the cotton moist so your patient can watch the sprout grow. Or how about an avocado pit? Poke three or four toothpicks around the top of the wide end of the pit. Place in a glass filled with water so that the bottom two-thirds of the pit is submerged in the water.

> Encourage those who are timid.
> Take tender care of those who are weak.
> Be patient with everyone.
>
> 1 Thessalonians 5:14, NLT

Homemade Medicine for the Spirit

This medicine for the spirit can encourage a patient of any age.

- Cut narrow four-inch strips of colored paper.
- Write on each paper a personal word of encouragement, a Bible verse, an "I love you because...," or even a joke.
- Roll up each strip of paper as tightly as possible. Drop a tiny spot of rubber cement on the end and wrap it with a twist tie or rubber band. When the rubber cement dries, remove the twist tie or rubber band.
- Fill a small box or large jar with these medicinal scrolls for the soul. Instruct the patient to "take one every four hours, three times a day."

you're the best

Take 1 every 4 hrs 3 times a day

> Now may the God of hope fill you with all joy and peace in believing, so that you will abound in hope by the power of the Holy Spirit.
>
> Romans 15:13, NASB

Sample messages:

"You're the best sister a guy could have. I love you!"

"When you get well, use this as a gift certificate for an ice-cream cone anyplace you choose!"

"Thanks for all the times you've helped me with my math. I'm glad you're so smart!"

"The LORD is my light and my salvation—whom shall I fear? The LORD is the stronghold of my life—of whom shall I be afraid?" (Psalm 27:1)

"Cast all your anxiety on God because he cares for you." (1 Peter 5:7)

"Surely I am with you always, to the very end of the age." (Matthew 28:20)

Box Party

Cards are nice on special occasions—but why stop there?

Bake some cookies or sweet bread, wrap them carefully, and put them in a box for mailing. Add colorful party napkins, a drink mix, paper cups, a package of confetti, noisemakers, and maybe a little something you picked out for the person you're honoring!

Wrap the box in paper that reflects the occasion (Birthday? Anniversary? Just for fun?). Then add a card explaining that you've sent an instant party!

Wrap it all to meet post office regulations, and your gift of love is ready to be on its way!

As we have opportunity, let us do good to all people, especially to those who belong to the family of believers.

Galatians 6:10

A Five-Course Birthday Party

If you end up going out to dinner for a birthday celebration, don't leave any of the fun at home. Take the presents with you! If the honoree is old enough and/or patient enough, have her open one gift after each step of the meal—one after ordering, one after beverages are served, one after the salad eaters get their salads, one after the main course, and, if there are any left, one after dessert. This is a great way to extend both aspects of birthday fun—the present opening and the shared meal. One more thing: Don't be surprised if the servers join in the fun by singing "Happy Birthday" with you or by offering a version of their own for your special guest.

"Blessed is the man who will eat at the feast in the kingdom of God."

Luke 14:15, NIV

Honorary Weekend for the "Distinguished"

At the beginning of each new year, designate one weekend during the coming twelve months for each child. On his or her weekend, that child can choose the activities he or she enjoys—backpacking, fishing, bicycling, skating, visiting the zoo—within any parameters you define. When your children are older, they will have a storehouse of wonderful memories from these special family weekends.

> Live...godly lives in this present age, while we wait for the blessed hope— the glorious appearing of our great God and Savior, Jesus Christ....
>
> Titus 2:12-13

- What would be a special "Good morning!" for the birthday person? Pancakes? Sugary cereal—just this once? Breakfast in bed? Not having to cook breakfast? If you're not sure, ask in advance!
- Choose one present to put at the birthday person's place at the breakfast table to be opened as soon as the special day begins!
- Mark the height of the birthday boy or girl on the garage wall or bathroom doorjamb—wherever you started that tradition. And if you haven't started that tradition, do so now!
- What does the birthday person want for dinner? Make his or her favorites!
- Before dessert or while you're eating the birthday cake, ask everyone at the table to offer an encouraging word about the person being honored: "Jon has sure become a much more confident reader"; "Sherry has worked hard all year at her free throws, and it's really paying off"; "I'm glad that Katie is making more time to read her Bible"; "Collin is being a lot kinder to his little sister"; "I'm glad Dad is my dad because I can talk to him about anything"; or "Mom's the best because she always knows just when I need a hug."
- Videotape an annual birthday interview of your growing child. Ask about special memories from the year. Be ready with prompts about happy times…challenges overcome…fun things that happened…accomplishments at school, in sports, in dance or music…and other meaningful moments. Add to this recording every year at birthday time! After the interview, play back the conversations from earlier birthdays and enjoy!

There's Something "Half-Way" Going On Here!

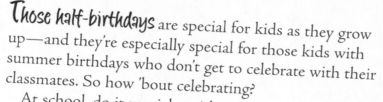

Those half-birthdays are special for kids as they grow up—and they're especially special for those kids with summer birthdays who don't get to celebrate with their classmates. So how 'bout celebrating?

At school, do it up right with cupcakes or ice-cream sandwiches for the class. Your half-birthday person might like to give a book to the class library or school library. Be sure to have the honoree sign and date the gift.

At home, why not celebrate with half a birthday cake? You could lead up to that with the half-birthday person's favorite meal and then surprise her with a unique half-dessert (that's still enough to feed everyone around the table, of course!).

Add half a glass of punch or sparkling cider and give the honoree half the money needed for a desired toy—and let her earn the rest. You might even try leaving out every other word while you sing "Happy Birthday."

From the fullness of his grace we have
all received one blessing after another.

John 1:16

Girl Time

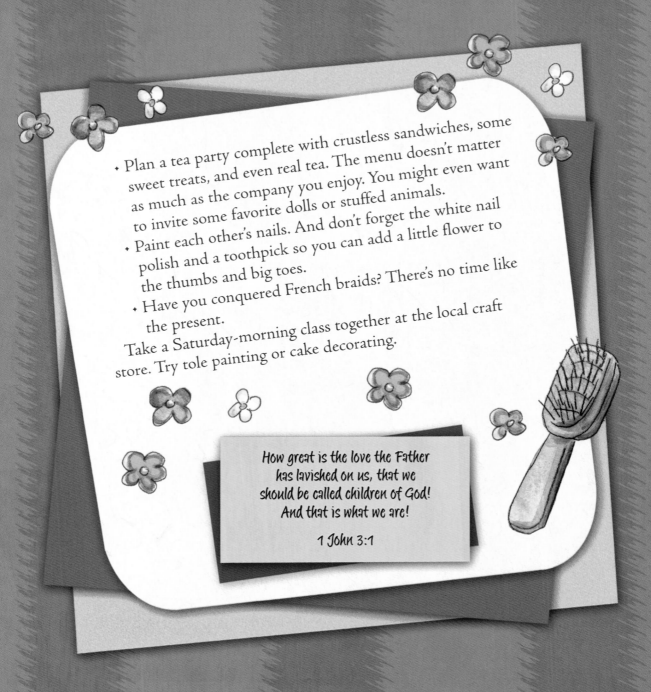

• Plan a tea party complete with crustless sandwiches, some sweet treats, and even real tea. The menu doesn't matter as much as the company you enjoy. You might even want to invite some favorite dolls or stuffed animals.

• Paint each other's nails. And don't forget the white nail polish and a toothpick so you can add a little flower to the thumbs and big toes.

• Have you conquered French braids? There's no time like the present.

Take a Saturday-morning class together at the local craft store. Try tole painting or cake decorating.

How great is the love the Father
has lavished on us, that we
should be called children of God!
And that is what we are!

1 John 3:1

A Thirteenth Birthday Befitting Her

+ Invite all the women in the family to join in the festivities.
+ Choose a fine china plate you'd like to pass on to your daughter, or purchase a new one. Dedicate the verse 2 Timothy 2:21, TLB, by writing the verse on the back of the plate, along with her name and the year.
+ Arrange ahead of time with the restaurant to have flowers brought to the table and sparkling cider served in crystal glasses, and to have them serve the birthday girl her dinner on the fine china plate.
+ Mom and the birthday girl start the special day by getting a manicure and pedicure together. It's a great way to get ready for and excited about going to a nice restaurant for dinner with the ladies.
+ To celebrate this passage from girl to young woman, encourage her understanding of how special she is in God's Kingdom and that some day God wants to use her for his highest purposes.
+ Add to this day any of your own traditions your family might do.

If you stay away from sin you will be like one of these dishes made of purest gold—the best in the house—so that Christ himself can use you for his highest purposes.
2 Timothy 2:21, TLB

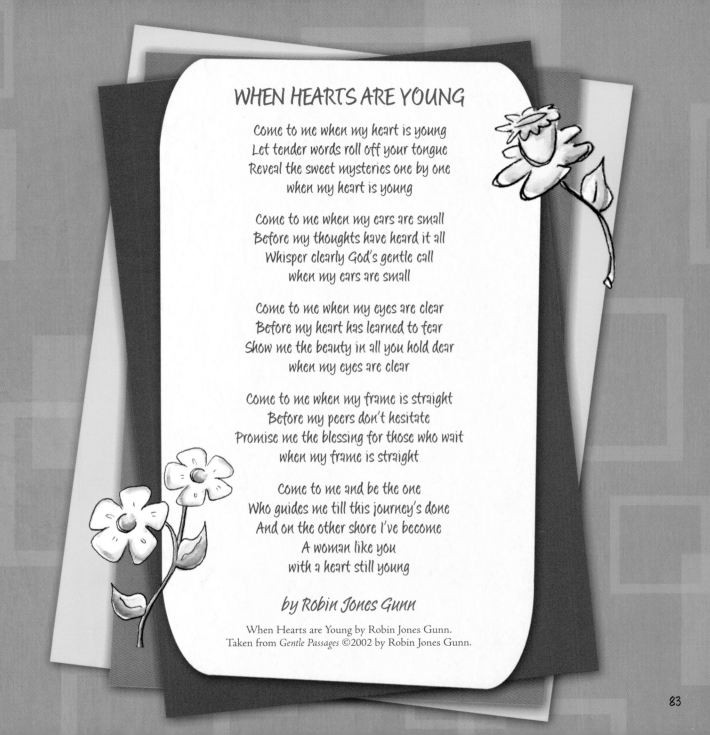

WHEN HEARTS ARE YOUNG

Come to me when my heart is young
Let tender words roll off your tongue
Reveal the sweet mysteries one by one
when my heart is young

Come to me when my ears are small
Before my thoughts have heard it all
Whisper clearly God's gentle call
when my ears are small

Come to me when my eyes are clear
Before my heart has learned to fear
Show me the beauty in all you hold dear
when my eyes are clear

Come to me when my frame is straight
Before my peers don't hesitate
Promise me the blessing for those who wait
when my frame is straight

Come to me and be the one
Who guides me till this journey's done
And on the other shore I've become
A woman like you
with a heart still young

by Robin Jones Gunn

When Hearts are Young by Robin Jones Gunn.
Taken from *Gentle Passages* ©2002 by Robin Jones Gunn.

Guy Time

- When was the last time you boys took some swings in the batting cages, visited the local trout pond, or took in a baseball game?
- Why not whip up an omelet or chocolate chip pancakes together for a Saturday morning breakfast?
- What around-the-house project (ideally, one that involves dirt, noise, and a bit of danger) will be more fun if you boys tackle it together?
- Can some one-on-one time become a productive lesson in bike maintenance or car maintenance? In gardening or sprinkler systems?

You have made known to me the path of life;
you fill me with joy in your presence....

Psalm 16:11

- If you live fairly close to the ocean, how about chartering a boat and going saltwater fishing? Don't forget to take the measuring tape and the video camera so there's no fudging on the size of the catch! Besides, it will be great fun to watch, again and again, the very moment when Andrew caught his first albacore.

- Head to the woods and go camping with Grandpa, Dad, the boys...and how 'bout Uncle Joe? While sitting around the fire eating s'mores, have a contest to see who tells the best story—Grandpa, Dad, or Uncle Joe. (We bet Grandpa could tell a few good ones about Dad and Joe that you've never heard before!)

- Any day when there is spiritual growth in a man's or a boy's life is a special day. So what about attending a men's retreat together? What a perfect opportunity to celebrate spiritual growth and the family's heritage of faith. There's nothing better or more important than passing down our spiritual heritage to the next generation. The retreat could also be a great occasion to present your son with his very first leather-bound Bible. Be sure to have his name inscribed in gold lettering.

May the God who gives endurance and encouragement give you a spirit of unity among yourselves as you follow Christ Jesus....

Romans 15:5

Welcome to the Family

Whether it's for a baby, an adult, or someone in between, baptism is an event worth celebrating.

- Be sure to attend the worship service. It's important to stand with the person being baptized or the parents and promise to help them or their child grow in a personal relationship with the Lord.
- What will you do to help disciple this person? Give the gift of that promise in writing.
- Consider the gift of a book—a children's Bible, a C. S. Lewis classic, a devotional, or anything else—that has been key in your walk with Jesus.
- Have a construction-paper tree trunk and branches hanging on a wall. Next to it have green leaves and markers so that your guests can write a favorite and appropriate Bible verse on it and then tape it to the tree.
- The celebration time might include committing to praying for the person on a long-term basis. After all, isn't prayer the best gift possible?

One day when the crowds were being baptized, Jesus himself was baptized. As he was praying, the heavens opened, and the Holy Spirit descended on him in the form of a dove.

Luke 3:21-22, NLT

How 'bout a Happy Holy Birthday!

A person's spiritual birthday is definitely worth celebrating. And if someone you love isn't quite sure of the date, let her choose a day that, each year, will be a touchstone of her faith journey.

- Every year, celebrate the day that person named Jesus as his Lord and Savior and became a member of God's forever family. You wouldn't skip a birthday celebration, so don't skip this one, either.
- Let the person choose what meal she'd like for dinner and, of course, what she'd like for dessert.
- Do special things to honor that person throughout the day, Make cards for him...find an appropriate book or journal from the local Christian bookstore...choose and dedicate a verse that pertains to whatever is going on in his spiritual walk that year...and, of course, make time to pray for her, to thank God that she knows Him and to ask His blessings on her walk with Him.

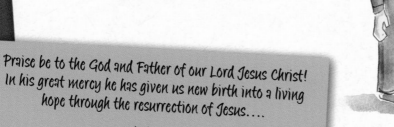

Praise be to the God and Father of our Lord Jesus Christ! In his great mercy he has given us new birth into a living hope through the resurrection of Jesus....

1 Peter 1:3

The Gift of a Parent's Blessing

Years ago, when our oldest daughter, Kari, was three years old, it took three tries one night to get her to bed. First came stories and prayers. Then a glass of water. Then her blanket had fallen on the floor. Just when we thought she was down for the night, her voice rang down the hallway.

"'Night, Mom. 'Night, Dad. And don't forget to bless me in the morning!"

At three years old, Kari was looking forward to something that children have longed for since Old Testament times…their parents'"blessing."

For us, it's been a morning event for Kari and her sister, Laura, each day of their lives. Not an elaborate ritual. Not something complicated or confusing. Just five simple steps outlined in God's Word.

If you'd like to leave the memory of a blessing in your child's life, then in your own way and words, pattern a specific time, morning or night, when you share five elements with your child.

First, meaningful touch. In Genesis 27, Isaac (whose son was over forty years) began his blessing with a hug and kiss before he spoke a word. For you, it may be lifting your children onto your lap, holding their hands, or simply laying your hand on their shoulder.

Then comes the spoken message. In other words, you put into words a praise or prayer for them that they hear out loud. But what kinds of words? Words that attach high value to the child. Isaac used a word picture of a field the Lord had blessed to give his son a picture of how valuable he was to him. Children need our appropriate touch and spoken words of love that attach high value to that child. And what's more, those words used to bless can help build a bright, shining future for a child when we use a fourth element of the blessing, special future. Children tend to be literalists when their parents speak positive or negative predictions for their life. When we praise a strength they have or pray for God's best for their future, we are giving them this fourth element of the blessing.

And finally, the blessing becomes real when it's linked with genuine commitment. It should be a deliberate action, like taking time to say to your child with your touch, words, and attitude, "Of all the kids in the world…I'd choose you."

What did Kari receive that next morning? A blessing as old as Abraham but as current as your home or mine. And while the words change each morning, her blessing that particular morning probably went much like this:

Lord, may You bless Kari today. And may You help her to know how much You love her and what a wonderful future You have for her. Thank You for how good she is at helping Mom with sister, Laura, and for how kind and strong she's becoming. And may she always know that we love her, Lord. Amen.

The blessing isn't a formula, but it does have specific ingredients: It's spoken in love. Shared with our hand on hers or our arms around her. And inspired by God's love, which we desire to communicate to her. That's a recipe for building a positive future in any child's life!

by John Trent

Picnic, Anyone?

Make a meal an adventure for any occasion. Here are some ideas:

- Mark the first official day of summer with an early evening picnic of chicken and cole slaw, biscuits and beans.
- A picnic by a lake or at sunset (or both) can add romance to any day—and either a husband or wife can arrange this.
- Have a "Good-Bye, Summer" picnic lunch the day before the kids start a new school year.
- Save some money and make some memories when you go to a ball game by having a tailgate party in the parking lot. The meal can be as simple or elaborate as you like.
- Do a potluck picnic with friends from the neighborhood, from church, or from work.
- Want some alone time with your middle child...your almost-teenage-and-growing-quiet son...your youngest who too easily gets lost in the shuffle? Pack a picnic lunch and go have some fun.

He directed the people to sit down on the grass. Taking the five loaves and the two fish and looking up to heaven, he gave thanks and broke the loaves. Then he gave them to the disciples, and the disciples gave them to the people.

Matthew 14:19

Thanks, Coach!

There are lots of ways to thank a coach when the season ends. Consider sharing photos from the season. Make a collage of action shots. In a note, thank the coach for helping you make specific improvements in your playing skill and ability. Let your coach know, too, that you appreciated any positive traits he modeled during the season (patience, good sportsmanship, an encouraging spirit, etc.). Acknowledge the coach's gift of time with something like movie passes or a kid-friendly restaurant gift certificate that he can enjoy with his whole family.

You're the Best!

I always thank God for you because of his grace given you in Christ Jesus.

1 Corinthians 1:4

CONGRATULATIONS, GRADUATE

Each of the milestones listed below is definitely cause for celebration. A special meal is always appropriate, and it may even be the setting for some of the following ways of both affirming the person you care about and noting his or her accomplishments. Spiritual growth, academic accomplishments, athletic efforts, participation in music and drama, a maturing character (more responsible, compassionate, respectful, etc.)—all these and more are worth affirming. Also, don't miss these opportunities to thank God for His faithfulness to the graduate and to pray for the graduate's future.

> Come, my children, listen to me;
> I will teach you the fear of the LORD.
> Psalm 34:11

Kindergarten Conquered

Of course, this once-in-a-lifetime moment is a photo op even if your young grad isn't wearing a mortarboard. And if he is, that photo will be great to compare to mortarboard shots in the future. Pull out your graduate's printing from early in the school year so she can see how much she's improved. Start an art gallery. Frame one or two favorite drawings in the clear (and inexpensive) acrylic frames available at a local craft store. What new school tool does a first grader need that a kindergartener didn't? Make a special occasion out of your trip to get that new lunch box or backpack or whatever.

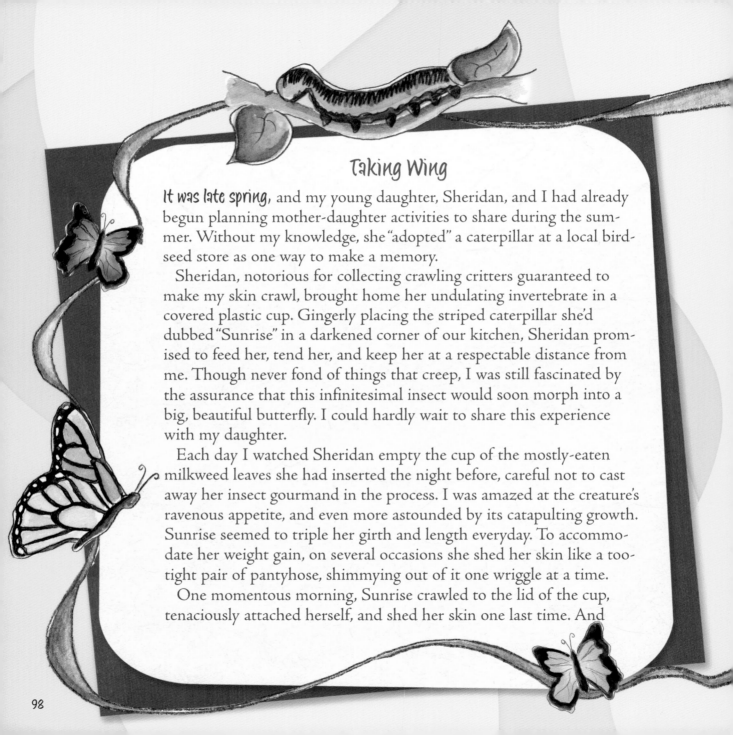

Taking Wing

It was late spring, and my young daughter, Sheridan, and I had already begun planning mother-daughter activities to share during the summer. Without my knowledge, she "adopted" a caterpillar at a local bird-seed store as one way to make a memory.

Sheridan, notorious for collecting crawling critters guaranteed to make my skin crawl, brought home her undulating invertebrate in a covered plastic cup. Gingerly placing the striped caterpillar she'd dubbed "Sunrise" in a darkened corner of our kitchen, Sheridan promised to feed her, tend her, and keep her at a respectable distance from me. Though never fond of things that creep, I was still fascinated by the assurance that this infinitesimal insect would soon morph into a big, beautiful butterfly. I could hardly wait to share this experience with my daughter.

Each day I watched Sheridan empty the cup of the mostly-eaten milkweed leaves she had inserted the night before, careful not to cast away her insect gourmand in the process. I was amazed at the creature's ravenous appetite, and even more astounded by its catapulting growth. Sunrise seemed to triple her girth and length everyday. To accommodate her weight gain, on several occasions she shed her skin like a too-tight pair of pantyhose, shimmying out of it one wriggle at a time.

One momentous morning, Sunrise crawled to the lid of the cup, tenaciously attached herself, and shed her skin one last time. And

then, in the stillness of that magical moment, she revealed a chrysalis of shimmering green and unseen dreams…and…she waited….

And so did we….

Over the ensuing weeks, Sheridan and I shared our hopes for the tiny tenant residing inside the chrysalis. And in the process, Sheridan began sharing her own hopes and dreams with me.

One day, in the fullness of time, we beheld a brilliant butterfly, her orange-and-black, stained-glass wings trembling inside the cup. We, too, trembled at her breathtaking beauty and at the thought of letting her go. Mustering our courage, we took Sunrise to the garden to free her, praying she'd linger among the lilacs yet a little while. She circled above the purple petals then suddenly flew to the treetops. Alighting for just an instant, she fluttered her wings like little rays of sunshine flashing on the black branches. Then she ascended higher still and finally disappeared from our sight.

Sheridan and I knew that we could never replace Sunrise, but we decided to adopt a new caterpillar every spring and raise it together. And I promised God that I would nurture my own little butterfly, whose childhood was flitting away with great speed—and that one day I would love her enough to let her take wing, just as we had done for Sunrise.

by Lynn D. Morrissey

Another School Year Under the Belt

The completion of every school year is worth noting.

- Take a picture of your sensational students.

- Bake a "Happy Summer!" cake! How 'bout a two-layer round cake with yellow frosting to welcome the sunny time of year?

- Make a list of things you want to do over your summer break—and *do* some of them.

- Compare a writing sample or handwriting from the first month of school to a sample from the last. Keep all these in a binder, so that your special student can see her improvement through the years.

Katie

Katie

- Update or add to that art gallery. (See "Kindergarten Conquered.")

- Make your own memory book for the school years or buy one and fill in the blanks. Whichever option you choose, include a school photo of your child, the teacher's name, and information about your child's favorites (for instance, a book he read during the year, a subject she enjoyed in school, a field trip he loved, school-year activities that she participated in, and any athletics they were involved in). Who were some of your child's pals? What was her favorite meal or snack or candy bar? What current events that happened during the school year are worth noting?

May his miracles have a deep
and permanent effect upon your lives!
Tell your children...
about the glorious miracles he did.

Deuteronomy 4:9, TLB

Elementary School: Mission Accomplished

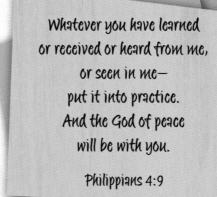

Whatever you have learned
or received or heard from me,
or seen in me—
put it into practice.
And the God of peace
will be with you.

Philippians 4:9

The foundation for a life of learning has been laid. Let a poster tell your favorite grad how proud you are. On a long piece of butcher paper or a sturdy poster board, use construction-paper bricks to build a house or frame a building with construction-paper pieces of wood. On each brick or board write a reason you're proud of your graduate: "You persevered and learned those multiplication tables"; "I'm so glad you reached out to the new students at your school"; "Teachers always commented that you were a joy to have in class"; "Good job working hard right through to the end"; "I'm so glad you discovered the world of books!"; "I wish I knew our state's history as well as you do." Don't just focus on accomplishments; let your comments affirm the person.

It's time for a special affirmation book. Have family members, friends, Sunday school teachers, significant teachers, important coaches, special neighbors, and anyone else who loves your graduate submit a single 8½" x 11" page to a book you'll put together. Give the contributors something more interesting than plain ol' white bond paper and invite them to share memories; a photo of themselves with the grad; "What I Like About You" thoughts; a favorite poem, saying, or Bible verse; or some encouraging words of wisdom. Compile these pages in a book that will be a friend to turn to during the tumultuous middle school years.

It's a photo op! And are you still updating your art gallery? Ask your grad what you can be praying for as she enters middle school.

Middle School Mastered

Middle school is like a sandwich, because it's what's in the middle that matters! What aspects of these middle school years provide you with opportunities to affirm your grad? Build a construction-paper sandwich on a piece of poster board or butcher paper and celebrate your middle school graduate. Write on each ingredient of the sandwich a highlight of the middle school years: "When I graduated from eighth grade, I sure hadn't conquered the math you already know"; "Your commitment to your daily Bible reading has been a powerful example for me"; "What a great science project you did in sixth grade. I'll always remember timing how long it took for the different brands of cornflakes to get soggy!"; "You were awesome in the school play!" Again, be sure to affirm the person, not just the accomplishments.

Are there any works of art to be framed? Any writing samples to be added to the collection from years gone by? Don't miss the photo op! Talk about the grad's plans and goals for high school. And be sure to ask your grad what you can be praying for as she enters high school.

Press on toward the goal for the prize of the upward call of God in Christ Jesus.

Philippians 3:14, NASB

Why not write your congratulatory affirmations on a white piece of paper made to look like a diploma? Or roll it up and tie it with a piece of ribbon like a scroll? Whatever the format, share words of encouragement: "It's clear that you are gifted in the area of music/math/history"; "You sure did a great job juggling all your commitments during high school"; "Just who taught you to play such a mean game of tennis?"; "I was proud of the way you hung in there with the one or two teachers who were hard to get along with"; "When can you teach me to be as organized as you are?"; "What a great GPA—but I'm even more pleased about your growth in the Lord"; "I can hardly wait to see what God has for you in college."

Again, any works of art you want to save? Any writing assignments you want to be sure to keep? Get a picture with that mortarboard in place. Ask your grad what you can be praying for as she heads for college. Talk about the graduate's goals. What help and/or encouragement can you offer? What Scripture verse or passage might be especially meaningful to your high school grad?

Fight the good fight of faith; take hold
of the eternal life to which you were called.

1 Timothy 6:12, NASB

College Completed

In a special note to the graduate, offer your perspective on her life. What strengths do you see? What growth can you point to? Which of his accomplishments are particularly significant? What challenges of life does she seem especially prepared for? Why is he important to you?

It's time for another mortarboard, so make sure the camera's in focus! Learn what the graduate's goals are. What help and/or encouragement can you offer? What Scripture verse or passage might be especially meaningful to your college graduate at this point in her life? Ask your grad what you can be praying for as he enters the workplace or goes to graduate school.

P.S. Is there a recording of "Pomp and Circumstance" available as background music for the festivities?

"For I know the plans I have for you,"
declares the LORD,
"plans to prosper you and not to harm you,
plans to give you hope and a future."

Jeremiah 29:11

The Songs of Spring: Easter Sunrise Service

Plan Ahead!

Take some time to find a quiet, pretty place where you can sit and watch the sun rise. Prepare a simple, carry-along breakfast of hard-boiled eggs, rolls, and juice. Don't forget your Bible so you can read the Easter story together. You might even want to bring song sheets to sing some Easter hymns. (How can you celebrate Easter without singing "Christ the Lord Is Risen Today"?!)

Alleluia... He is Risen

Christ the Lord is risen today, Alleluia!
Earth and heaven in chorus say, Alleluia!
Raise your joys and triumph high, Alleluia!
Sing, ye heavens, and earth reply, Alleluia! (vs.1)
Soar we now where Christ has led, Alleluia!
Following our exalted Head, Alleluia!
Made like him, like him we rise, Alleluia!
Ours the cross, the grave, the skies, Alleluia! (vs. 4)

> His appearance was like lightning,
> and his clothes were white as snow.
> Matthew 28:3

He Is Risen!

Get up early enough to get to your special place just before the sun comes up. Spread out a blanket to sit on. Then read together about the women going to Jesus' tomb and what happened when they arrived (Matthew 28:1–15). As the sun comes up over the horizon, sing a joyous song of victory! Then thank God for the gift of Jesus and His triumph over sin and death! Thank Him for the promise and hope of eternal life! Celebrate by sharing the simple breakfast you've brought with you.

Resurrection Buns

Just like the tomb on Easter Sunday, these tasty buns are empty on the inside! Enjoy!

1 package Rhodes frozen Rolls
24 large marshmallows
1/4 cup (1/2 stick) melted butter or margarine
1/2 cup sugar mixed with 1/2 teaspoon cinnamon

Thaw 24 rolls. Flatten each roll to about 3" in diameter. Place a large marshmallow in the center of the dough and pinch dough together to seal the marshmallow inside. Roll between the palms of your hands into the size of a golf ball. Dip in the melted butter, then roll in the cinnamon-sugar and place on a lightly greased cookie sheet spaced apart evenly. Let rise until double in size (30 to 60 minutes). Bake at 350° F for 15 to 20 minutes, until golden brown. Remove from the cookie sheet and cool on a wire rack.

Fairy Tale

I'd waited so long. My three closest friends were not only married, but two of them had children with their own e-mail accounts. Since I'd shared questions and frustrations with audiences across the nation, I'd heard every rationale known to, well, man. Believers everywhere were praying that I would defy the odds and stymie the statistics. I guess God had to do *something*.

Following a string of events best described as "God things," I found myself with a bridal gown in alterations, a string quartet on retainer, and a rehearsal dinner featuring an entrée I couldn't pronounce. Our first date was in December and we would marry in July. I was *still* shaking my head.

The wedding was beautiful. The sprawling Southern plantation home proved perfect for this intimate celebration: hardwood floors, spiral staircase, wraparound porch, pillars, arbor, and, of course, a staid magnolia in front. The florist used atypical flowers and greenery, giving the rooms a distinct, unique look. The catering was superb. The string quartet was very nice, and while they struggled on the wedding march (can you say "train wreck"?), the classical pieces were performed beautifully.

On cue, I descended the staircase with my sister in the lead and my bridal train in tow. When the room came into full view, I realized that what was most important to me were not the flowers, the food, or the music. It was the faces. Friends had come from twelve states—not to see a writer or a performer, but simply to celebrate this day with us. They'd rearranged work schedules, made travel arrangements, and spent two days here for a twenty-minute ceremony that would have been no less valid had they not come at all—less memorable, for certain, but no less legitimate.

It's interesting…when singing very emotional songs I remain poised and have often been touted for my composure; however, when we began exchanging vows, I realized that God was making a dream come true and I was standing right in the middle of it! I blubbered, I sniffed, I couldn't even speak. God had remembered the petitions of my heart. He had helped me forge lifelong friendships with these whose faith was more stubborn than mine; then He'd bent to hear their supplication on my behalf. On that hot Saturday in July, God was with us…again.

At dinner some weeks afterward, John's best man and his wife presented to us a picture they'd taken at the rehearsal dinner. The lovely frame was engraved with words similar to what He'd been suggesting to us all along: "Once in a while, right in the middle of an ordinary life, love gives us a fairy tale."

Well said.

by Janet Paschal

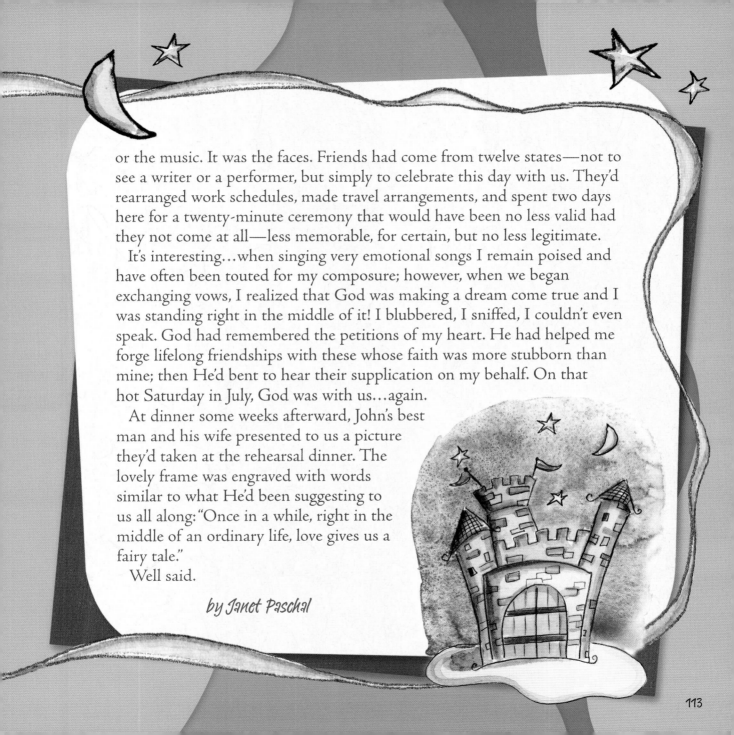

Summertime Is Family Reunion Time

Does the second Saturday of August or the third Sunday in July work for you? Make it the same date every year.

- Reserve a good spot for picnics in advance and then let everyone know how to get to it and when to be there.
- Make it a potluck. Have everyone bring a favorite recipe or one they're famous for. Maybe this year Aunt Loretta will bring two custard pies so folks don't have to fight for a slice. (Although scheming for a slice is part of the fun!)
- Choose a different theme each year.
- Want crazy centerpieces for a farmer theme? Make a special flower arrangement to place on a red-and-white-checkered tablecloth. Use craft foam for the flowers and pipe cleaners for the stems. Then crop and paste last summer's "reject" photos onto the center of the flowers. (Only use photos of folks who can laugh when they see themselves with their eyes closed, barbecue sauce dripping down their chin, or covered with goop after the egg toss.)
- Appoint a family photographer. (This honor can be passed along from year to year.) Have that person bring binders of the family reunion photos to the following year's reunion.
- It wouldn't be a picnic without an egg- or water-balloon toss. And yes, adults participate!
- What about a hula hoop contest? And of course you need a football or two to pass back and forth.
- Bingo works, too! Don't forget the prizes.
- Plan ahead for the talent show of family skits, music, poems, jokes, whatever! Again, all ages are included.

- What special event can highlight your family heritage? If you're a Scottish clan, have a bagpiper come. If you're German, take time to teach the younger generation the polka. If you're Irish, ask some local dancers to perform for you. If you're Greek, be sure to have some baklava to share.
- The grand finale could be the Family Presentation. The eldest member in attendance introduces the entire family to everyone attending. Everyone is introduced and, yes, it can be embarrassing. (Why doesn't Mom get our names straight?) But it's a great photo op and a way to meet new babies and new spouses.
- One more detail: Have a bucket on hand for donations for the next reunion. The funds cover the costs of mailing invitations and reserving the park.

Let us not give up meeting together...
but let us encourage one another—
and all the more as you see the Day approaching.

Hebrews 10:25

The stars tell us something very, very important. As David the psalmist said, "The heavens declare the glory of God" (Psalm 19:1). Plan an evening under the stars to see if you agree!

Pick a nice, clear evening, head outside, and look up. Better yet, lie down on a blanket and, depending on the temperature, even under a blanket.

What do those sparkling stars reveal to you about the God who created them? Think, for instance, about how strong or big God must be.

Do you see the Big Dipper, the North Star, Orion, or Cassiopeia? What do constellations like these reveal about the universe? (Hint: Is there anything accidental or random about the way the stars are arranged?)

Take a few minutes to look at the moon. How much of it do you see? How bright is it? And, kids, ask your parents this riddle: How is the moon like a Christian? (Hint: Both reflect the sun's/Son's light!) Take a few minutes to brainstorm what you can do as a family to reflect the light of Jesus at your school and in your neighborhood.

Isn't it amazing that such a mighty, creative, and awesome God knows you by name and even numbers the hairs on your head? (Matthew 10:30). Spend a few minutes praising God for the beauty of His creation. His love for you is immeasurable...it's a love that reaches "higher than the heavens" (Psalm 108:4)!

Take time for a family hug before you head inside, and then everyone drink a cup of hot Sleepytime tea or apple cider before you call it a night.

SWEET DREAMS!

Is not God in the heights of heaven?
And see how lofty are the highest stars!
Job 22:12

Winter Wonderland

Does it snow in the winter where you live? Consider renting a horse and sleigh. Load up the kids with lots of blankets and hand warmers and off you go. Sing songs...look for fresh animal tracks in the snow...talk about winters past...watch for birds flying in the wintry sky...and plan to thaw your frozen bones with hot cocoa and gingerbread cake enjoyed by the fire.

(Don't forget to bring some carrots to reward the horse for all his hard work!)

- The family that skates together...plops together. But most of us have enough built-in padding that no one gets hurt, and the tumbles are great for some fun and laughs. So, if you have access to a rink or a frozen pond, give ice skating a whirl. Skating hand in hand to oldies or playing chase on the ice is a wonderful way to celebrate the winter season and have fun together. In fact, you just might end up starting a new family tradition.

House-Blessing Celebration

Are you building a home? Then have a house-blessing party. Hand out permanent markers to the people you invite and ask them to write blessings or Scripture verses on the foundation of the new house. Be sure to take pictures before the carpet is laid. Also, it's wonderful to pray beforehand for the activities that will happen in each room.

Fix these words of mine in your hearts and minds; Write them on the doorframes of your houses and on your gates....

Deuteronomy 11:18, 20

120

121

Farewell Memories for Moving Day

Are you saying good-bye to a much-loved home?
After the moving van has left but before you hand over the keys, order out for pizza and have it delivered. In a favorite spot, share pizza and memories of all the life you lived in that house. Thank God for the good times as well as for the hard times that He used for your good.

New Home Prayer Walk

Are you moving into a new home? Then do a variation on the house-blessing party. Invite a handful of praying friends over and take a prayer walk through the house. In each room pray for the specific activities that will take place in that room and for the particular individuals associated with that room: "Bless JoAnn with the gift of hospitality. As she prepares meals and opens her new home to people, may they know Your love through her love"; "May this room be a place where You meet Dennis and grow him to be more the young man of God that You want him to be"; "Lord, please make this family room a place rich in laughter and love." OPTIONAL: It also never hurts to pray for God's Holy Spirit to blow through the house and cleanse it from whatever practices and activities have happened before within its walls.

"Listen to the cry and to the prayer which
Your servant prays before You today;
that Your eyes may be open toward this house night
and day, toward the place of which You have said,
'My name shall be there,' to listen to the prayer
which Your servant shall pray toward this place."

1 Kings 8:28-29, NASB